TELEVISION

FROM CONCEPT TO CONSUMER

BY STEVEN

CHILDREN'S PRESS®

An Imprint of Scholastic Inc.
New York   Toronto   London   Auckland   Sydney
Mexico City   New Delhi   Hong Kong
Danbury, Connecticut

CONTENT CONSULTANT
Hugh Haynie, Executive Producer, Radiate Media

PHOTOGRAPHS ©: Alamy Images: 29 right (AF archive), 51 (Anthony Brown), 40 (Aurora Photos), 10 left, 10 right, 11 left (Everett Collection Inc), 30 (Francis Vachon), 46 (fStop), 8, 14 (INTERFOTO), 25 right (Juice Images), 35 (keith morris), 22 (Marmaduke St. John), 24 left (photonic 7), 47 (SuperStock), 28 right, 29 left (White House Photo), 34 (ZUMA Press, Inc.); AP Images: 5 right, 55 (Bob Luckey/Greenwich Time), 48 (Dan Steinberg/Invision), 39 (David Goldman), 24 right, 25 left (Fang Yingzhong/Color China Photo), 49 (Frank Micelotta/Invision), 23 (Reed Saxon), 42 (Richard Drew), 54 (Scott Gries/Invision), 53 (Seth Wenig), 16, 28 left; Corbis Images/Bettmann: 4 left, 9, 12; Everett Collection: 26 (HBO), 31 (Mike Yarish/©Netflix), 13, 15 top, 15 bottom; Getty Images: 11 right (Allan Grant), 17, 18, 44 (CBS Photo Archive), 52 (DreamPictures); Hugh Haynie: 36, 37 top, 37 bottom; Media Bakery: 5 left, 32, 38, 44 (Digital Vision), 59 (Frank van Delft), 58 (i love images), 41 (Jorge Cruz), 56 (Mark Hunt), 27 (Pop! Studio Photography), 3, 43 (Ron Nickel), 4 right, 20 (Simon Marcus), 20 (Stuart Pearce), 50 (Tim Pannell); Shutterstock, Inc.: 57 (Monkey Business Images), cover (Sergey Nivens); The Image Works: 6 (Classicstock), 19 (SSPL).

LIBRARY OF CONGRESS CATALOGING-IN-PUBLICATION DATA
Otfinoski, Steven.
  Television : from concept to consumer / by Steven Otfinoski.
    pages cm. — (Calling all innovators: a career for you?)
  Includes bibliographical references and index.
  ISBN 978-0-531-20612-6 (library binding) — ISBN 978-0-531-21071-0 (pbk.)
  1. Television broadcasting—Juvenile literature. 2. Television—Vocational guidance—Juvenile literature. I. Title.
  PN1992.57074 2014
  384.55—dc23   2014003567

2 3 4 5 6 7 8 9 10 R 24 23 22 21 20 19 18 17 16 15 14

Science, technology, engineering, arts, and math are the fields that drive innovation. Whether they are finding ways to make our lives easier or developing the latest entertainment, the people who work in these fields are changing the world for the better. Do you have what it takes to join the ranks of today's greatest innovators? Read on to discover whether television is a career for you.

TABLE *of* CONTENTS

Philo Farnsworth was the inventor of the first all-electronic television.

CHAPTER ONE

Television Through Time............ 7

CHAPTER TWO

Television Today 21

Today, huge flat-screen TVs are a common sight in living rooms around the world.

A television crew prepares to broadcast a news program.

CHAPTER THREE

Careers in Television 33

AN INTERVIEW WITH

Television Producer Hugh Haynie 36

CHAPTER FOUR

From Idea to Broadcast ... 45

Crew members use headsets to stay in touch as they film a show.

CAREER STATS 60
RESOURCES 61
GLOSSARY 62
INDEX 63
ABOUT THE AUTHOR 64

CONTROL KNOBS FOR CHANGING CHANNELS AND VOLUME

BLACK-AND-WHITE SCREEN

Early television sets are almost unrecognizable next to today's wide, flat screens.

CHAPTER ONE

TELEVISION THROUGH TIME

I magine you're sitting in your living room one rainy afternoon. You're bored stiff with nothing to do, so you turn on the TV. A black-and-white film comes on. It's not exactly the greatest movie you've ever seen, so you flip the channel to see what else is on. However, all of the other stations just show static. You switch back to the movie and watch the rest of it. Then comes another surprise. After the movie ends, the station goes off the air—at 5:00 p.m.!

You come back a couple of hours later and turn on your only channel. A hockey game is on. The action is hard to follow. One camera is trying to capture everything, and there are no slow-mo instant replays. There is no big screen to watch the action on either. Your TV screen is about the size of a folded napkin.

What's going on here? Are you on another planet? No, it's just the United States in the year 1940. Television is still in its earliest stages, and you're one of the few families in your neighborhood to own a television set!

EARLY TV LANDMARKS

1947	1948	1949	1950
John Cameron Swayze becomes the first major TV news **anchor** on the Camel News Caravan.	The Lone Ranger *becomes one of TV's first western series.*	*The first ever Emmy Awards are presented on January 25.*	*The popular game shows* Beat the Clock *and* What's My Line? *first appear.*

PIONEERS OF TELEVISION

The technology behind television dates back as far as the late 1800s. In the 1870s and 1880s, inventors around the world began experimenting with ways to send photographic images from one location to another using electronic signals. In 1884, German inventor Paul Nipkow designed a device called a Nipkow disk. The Nipkow disk was a spinning disk that could record an image line by line, from top to bottom. This process is known as scanning. Each line of a scanned image could be sent electronically to a receiving device in a different location. This receiver could then project the original image line by line onto a screen.

JOHN LOGIE BAIRD

Many inventors attempted to use Paul Nipkow's ideas to create working televisions. One of the first big successes finally came in 1925, when Scottish inventor John Logie Baird used television to transmit an image of a human face. The following year, Baird became the first person ever to televise a moving picture. Television as we know it today was born.

SPINNING DISK

The Nipkow disk helped lead to the creation of television as we know it today.

Philo Farnsworth shows off the inner workings of his all-electronic television receiver.

CATHODE RAY TUBE

RADIO RECEIVER

POWER SUPPLY

PHILO FARNSWORTH

In the 1920s, inventor Philo Farnsworth developed an all-electronic television. Farnsworth's invention relied on electronic signals instead of spinning disks to scan and transmit images. It created a sharper, smoother image than mechanical television could offer.

FROM INVENTION TO INDUSTRY

Television technology rapidly began to improve in the years following John Logie Baird's breakthrough. Radio Corporation of America (RCA) executive David Sarnoff realized the technology's potential. RCA put millions of dollars into developing the new technology. In 1930, it opened a television station that sent TV signals through the air using its radio network, which was called the National **Broadcasting** Company (NBC). People slowly began purchasing television sets for their homes. By the end of 1941, there were 21 TV stations in the United States. More than a million television sets had been sold. However, the United States' entry into World War II that December put a stop to television development for the next four years.

RCA's David Sarnoff (left) poses with radio inventor Guglielmo Marconi (right).

RADIO PAVES THE WAY

Television as we know it today would not exist without the development of radio. Radio was invented by Italian engineer Guglielmo Marconi in 1895. In the 1920s, it became the main source for news and entertainment in the United States. By 1933, two-thirds of American homes had at least one radio.

ADDING SIGHT TO SOUNDS

"Now we add sight to sound," RCA's David Sarnoff announced at the 1939 World's Fair in New York. More than a decade earlier, Sarnoff had founded NBC, the largest radio network in the country. Under Sarnoff, NBC expanded into television broadcasting. Because NBC already had the equipment to send signals

over the air, it was easy for the company to begin broadcasting television in addition to radio. The Columbia Broadcasting System (CBS) and the American Broadcasting Company (ABC) were also radio networks that developed into television networks.

David Sarnoff speaks to the press in front of the RCA pavilion at the 1939 World's Fair.

Richard Boone starred as the Wild West hero Paladin in Have Gun — Will Travel.

FROM RADIO TO TELEVISION

Nearly all the **genres** of television programs we know today began as radio shows. On radio programs, actors performed their lines as narrators explained the action. These shows included **sitcoms**, dramas, soap operas, variety shows, children's shows, talk shows, and news programs. During the 1950s, some shows had both radio and TV versions. One example is the western series *Have Gun — Will Travel.* While radio continues to entertain and inform today with music, news, and talk programs, television has become a far more popular form of entertainment. ☀

Comedian Milton Berle and singer Ethel Merman perform on an episode of Texaco Star Theater.

TV COAST TO COAST

In 1946, the year after World War II ended, RCA debuted its latest all-electronic television set. The new set could display images at a **resolution** of 630 lines. This produced the highest picture quality of any television yet. Viewers used their new TVs to watch the many shows that debuted in the postwar years. Among the most popular shows was the children's program *The Howdy Doody Show*, which starred a freckle-faced wooden puppet. The westerns *Hopalong Cassidy* and *The Lone Ranger* also drew large audiences. So did the first hit variety show, *Texaco Star Theater*, which featured comedian Milton Berle.

In television's early years, all programming was produced locally. People in different parts of the country saw different shows. But in 1951, a network of communications towers that could send TV signals across the entire nation was completed. On September 4, 1951, the first nationwide broadcast took place from San Francisco, California. It featured president Harry Truman.

THE GOLDEN AGE

That same year also saw the debut of the first hit sitcom, *I Love Lucy*. *I Love Lucy* was the first TV series to be filmed with multiple cameras in front of a live audience. Filmed episodes were sent across the country and broadcast by local stations. This remains the standard way most sitcoms are broadcast today.

By the mid-1950s, television entered what many people consider a "golden age." Many popular live dramatic series were aired during prime time hours of roughly 7:00 to 11:00 p.m., drawing huge audiences each evening. As the decade progressed, live programs were replaced more and more by filmed series that were less expensive to produce and could be shown many times in reruns. Major Hollywood studios such as Walt Disney and Warner Bros. began producing television shows in addition to theatrical films.

The zany characters of I Love Lucy *helped make it one of the most popular shows in TV history.*

EXPERIMENTS IN COLOR

Color television was first attempted by inventor John Logie Baird as early as 1928. CBS began broadcasting experimental color programs in 1940. Eventually, color television would completely replace the black-and-white images that early viewers enjoyed.

FROM LINES TO DOTS

The first television sets capable of displaying colored **pixels** were released by RCA in the late 1940s. RCA's color sets were expensive, and owners found it difficult to adjust the way the colors were displayed. When NBC's puppet show *Kukla, Fran and Ollie* became the first

Researchers experimented with color television technology for years before color TVs became common household products.

Kukla, Fran and Ollie *was created by puppeteer Burr Tillstrom.*

regular program to be broadcast in color in 1949, most viewers saw it in black and white. Most U.S. households did not have color television sets at the time.

IN LIVING COLOR

By 1965, color TVs remained rare in U.S. homes. But within a few years, color sets improved in quality and became less expensive, encouraging people to begin buying them in larger numbers. NBC's colorful peacock logo proudly announced it as the "color network." By 1972, the sales of color sets surpassed those of black-and-white sets for the first time. Today, there is at least one color television set in almost every U.S. home. ☀

NBC's brightly colored logo helped the network stand out in the early days of color TV.

CHANGING THE FACE OF POLITICS

The power of television to inform and influence American life became apparent in the 1960s. The first televised presidential debate took place on September 26, 1960. About 75 million viewers watched as candidates Richard Nixon and John F. Kennedy appeared on-screen to discuss the time's most important political issues. In earlier elections, voters had relied on written words and radio broadcasts to learn about candidates. The only way to see politicians in action was to attend speeches or rallies where they appeared in person. This time, voters would get the chance to see the candidates in motion from the comfort of their homes. During the debate, Kennedy seemed handsome and charming. Nixon, despite years of political experience, seemed like a far less appealing candidate. Voters witnessed him looking sickly, sweaty, and pale during the debate. In part because of this, Kennedy went on to win the election.

When the young president was tragically assassinated on November 22, 1963, Americans gathered around their television sets to watch hours upon hours of coverage over the next four days. Never before had so many people turned to television as a news source.

The televised fourth and final debate between John F. Kennedy and Richard Nixon on October 21, 1960, had a major effect on the results of that year's presidential election.

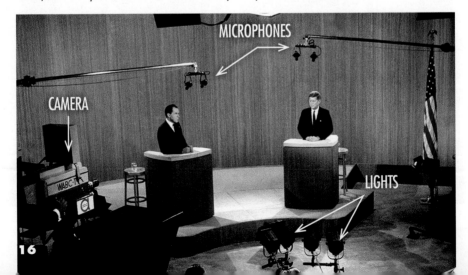

Broadcasting technology enabled journalists such as Walter Cronkite (center) to give viewers an up close look at global events such as the Vietnam War.

THE LIVING ROOM WAR

If Kennedy was the first "television president," then the Vietnam War was the first "television war." Footage direct from the warfront was aired nightly on evening news broadcasts. Most viewers had never seen war from such a graphic, close-up perspective. As a result, the war drew more criticism from American citizens than any previous conflict had.

With the rising number of people turning to television for their news updates, newscasters had also gained the power to help shape public opinion on current events. In early 1968, Walter Cronkite, a popular news anchor, ended a half-hour-long special on the war by stating his belief that it was unwinnable. President Lyndon Johnson is said to have shut off the program and told his advisors, "If I've lost Cronkite, I've lost middle America." Johnson was correct. Many voters agreed with Cronkite and did not support Johnson's decision to continue fighting the war. A little more than a month after Cronkite's special aired, Johnson announced that he would not run for a second term as president.

Gary Burghoff (left) and Alan Alda (right) were two of the stars of M*A*S*H.

GROWING UP

The 1970s saw a maturing of television programming. Many of the era's most popular shows dealt with real-life issues. *The Mary Tyler Moore Show* was about a young, unmarried woman with a career in television news. *M*A*S*H* was about doctors working on the front lines during the Korean War.

Viewers also began to get more options when it came to TV channels. Public television became a major competitor to the three commercial networks (ABC, NBC, and CBS) by offering excellent programming in the arts, sciences, and public affairs. The 1970s also saw the rise of **cable** TV. Instead of being sent through the air, cable programming was delivered through cable lines that plugged into TV sets. Cable networks such as Home Box Office (HBO) offered theatrical movies and special programming that couldn't be seen on network television.

CHOOSING WHAT TO WATCH

Videocassette recorders (VCRs) were first introduced in the 1970s. However, sales of these devices did not take off until the 1980s. VCRs allowed TV viewers to record programs onto tapes for later viewing. They also allowed people to watch prerecorded videotapes (usually movies) on their TV screens. TV viewing habits changed drastically. People no longer had to tune in at just the right time to see a favorite show. They could also fast-forward past commercials and other parts of a program that they didn't want to watch.

During the 1980s, more cable channels challenged the dominance of the three main networks. Many specialized in a certain type of programming instead of offering a wide variety. There were channels devoted to sports (ESPN), old movies (American Movie Classics), children's programming (Nickelodeon and the Disney Channel), and news (CNN). By 1989, 60 percent of American homes had cable. It was a huge change from the early days when there were few channels to choose from. In the years ahead, television would change even more.

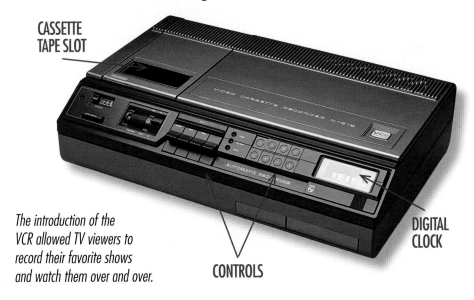

CASSETTE TAPE SLOT

DIGITAL CLOCK

CONTROLS

The introduction of the VCR allowed TV viewers to record their favorite shows and watch them over and over.

Modern televisions are much larger and offer far better picture quality than earlier versions of the technology.

CHAPTER TWO

TELEVISION TODAY

Today, television sets are used for far more than just watching broadcasts from a handful of major networks. They serve as central hubs for home entertainment centers that offer almost anything viewers could ever want to see, right in the comfort of the living room. There are hundreds upon hundreds of cable and **satellite** TV channels to choose from, and many TV sets allow viewers to watch more than one channel at a time. Cable companies have movies and TV shows "on demand," with a menu of available content to choose from. Video game consoles, Blu-ray discs, and DVDs expand the viewer's options to a nearly limitless range. Many viewers think there is almost too much entertainment to choose from, and thanks to the latest TV technology, it all looks bigger and better than ever.

TECHNICAL TRIUMPHS

1962	1964	1998	2007
The satellite Telstar relays the first programs between Europe and the United States.	The plasma screen is invented.	HDTV sets hit stores for the first time.	Netflix begins offering customers the option to stream video content over the Internet.

SATELLITE TV

Today, many households subscribe to satellite television providers. These services are especially useful for people who live in places where cable television is not offered. Satellite television first became a reality on July 23, 1962, when the satellite *Telstar* broadcast programming to the United States and Europe at the same time. Viewers on both sides of the Atlantic looked in awe as live images of New York's Statue of Liberty and Paris's Eiffel Tower were displayed side by side on the same TV screen.

Satellite TV providers send signals to a satellite 22,000 miles (35,406 kilometers) above Earth. The satellite then sends the signals back to Earth, directly to the subscribers' homes. The signals are received by a dish that subscribers can mount on a roof or alongside a house. The dish transports the signals to a receiver inside the home.

Satellite dishes are carefully installed and calibrated by trained professionals.

SIGNALS ARE PICKED UP BY RECEIVER

SATELLITE SIGNALS BOUNCE OFF OF DISH

People with older televisions must hook converter boxes up to their sets in order to watch digital broadcasts.

TELEVISION GOES DIGITAL

Until recently, television programming was sent to viewers using the same type of signals that networks had been using since the first TV stations began broadcasting. This is known as analog television. In the 1990s, researchers developed a new way of transmitting television signals. This is called digital television. The advantages of digital over analog are enormous. Digital signals can send more information at once than analog signals can. This means digital TV broadcasts can transmit high-definition (HD) pictures and sound. HD programming is displayed in very high resolution, which makes the image sharper and more lifelike. It also offers higher sound quality to viewers who have good audio systems.

At first, most viewers could not watch HD digital broadcasts because their old television sets could only receive analog signals. This all changed rapidly when HDTV sets decreased in price, and people began buying them in large numbers. By the mid-2000s, all networks were broadcasting digital HDTV signals, and analog TV was almost entirely a thing of the past in the United States.

MODERN MARVELS

PICTURE PERFECT

The rise of digital TV saw the need for bigger, better types of screens to display detailed HD images. For more than 75 years, cathode-ray tube (CRT) screens were the standard for television sets. However, CRT screens are heavy and bulky. This makes them impractical for large TV sets. Today, most TV sets use plasma or liquid crystal display (LCD) screens. These TVs offer picture quality far superior to CRT sets, and they are available in extremely large sizes.

Workers assemble LCD TVs at a factory in China.

The cathode-ray tubes that powered older televisions would not fit inside today's slim screens.

LIQUID CRYSTALS

LCD screens are made of two clear panels with a layer of liquid crystal material between them. Light is projected through the screen from behind. Electrical signals cause the liquid crystal layer to move and change. As a result, different parts of the screen allow different parts of light through. This creates the colors that make up the image on the screen.

WHICH ONE IS THE RIGHT ONE?

In most ways, it is difficult to tell plasma and LCD TVs apart. Both are thin and light enough to hang from walls, and both can display incredibly detailed images at huge sizes. However, there are pros and cons for each of the two TV types. For example, the picture on an LCD screen can sometimes be hard to see when viewed from an angle. Plasma TVs do not have this problem. On the other hand, LCD TVs can be much thinner and lighter than plasma TVs, and they use less electricity. It is up to buyers to decide which type of screen is right for them.

There are so many different styles and sizes of TVs available today that it can be difficult to choose which to buy.

THE MAGIC OF PLASMA

A plasma screen is made of two clear panels with a center layer of pixels between them. Instead of a light shining from behind the panels, as in an LCD screen, plasma TV pixels produce their own light. Each pixel is capable of displaying any color. TV signals tell the pixels which colors to display, and this produces the image on the screen.

The Sopranos *changed the way that many people thought about television dramas.*

A SECOND GOLDEN AGE

For many years, cable networks such as HBO and Showtime mostly aired recently released movies. During the 1990s, many of these channels began increasing the amount of original programming they broadcast. Unlike major networks such as CBS or NBC, cable channels did not have to follow U.S. laws about the type of content they broadcast. They were free to include violence, strong language, and other content not seen on network television. As a result, cable TV creators were free to make groundbreaking shows without worrying about **censorship**. This attracted top filmmaking talent to cable TV. Cable series, such as *The Sopranos*, offered high-quality acting, writing, and directing that made them more similar to Hollywood films than traditional television dramas. Today, cable hits such as *Mad Men*, *The Walking Dead*, and *Game of Thrones* are among the many series that follow in these shows' footsteps.

INTERNET TELEVISION

Today, you don't even need a TV set to watch some of your favorite shows. All you need is an Internet connection and computer, tablet, or other device. Starting in the 2000s, cable channels such as CNN and MTV began offering streaming video programming online. Today, almost every TV channel offers at least some sort of streaming content. Some channels allow viewers to watch live broadcasts that are exactly the same as what is shown on TV. Others offer clips and full episodes of popular shows that viewers can choose on demand. These services are perfect for people who are on the go or who don't have TV sets at home.

Today, you don't need to be in the living room to watch television shows.

FROM THIS TO THAT

The Beatles were introduced to U.S. fans when they first appeared on The Ed Sullivan Show *in 1964.*

UP ALL NIGHT

For more than 60 years, TV viewers have been staying up late to watch the unique blend of comedy, celebrity interviews, and music that is the late-night talk show. These wildly popular shows all have a few things in common. Each is hosted by a comedian who delivers jokes about news and current events, participates in comedic sketches, and interviews a wide variety of famous and interesting guests. Many shows also feature musical performances by popular artists.

THE EARLY DAYS

The ancestors of today's top talk shows are the variety shows aired by the networks during the earliest years of television. Popular programs such as *The Ed Sullivan Show* featured a wide range of performances, from pop musicians and stage actors to dancers and stand-up comics.

In 1954, NBC debuted *The Tonight Show*. Like modern talk shows, each episode opened with a monologue from the host and featured interviews with guests in addition to performances and sketches. *The Tonight Show* continues to air today and has been hosted by famous comedians, such as Steve Allen, Johnny Carson, and Jay Leno, throughout its history.

FROM NETWORKS TO CABLE

Because of their popularity and the relatively low cost to produce them, many new late-night talk shows appeared in the following decades. NBC, CBS, and ABC all developed their late-night series, with each show's host putting his or her own unique spin on the genre. Eventually, cable channels ranging from HBO to E! developed late-night talk shows of their own. For example, TBS's *Conan*, starring veteran NBC host Conan O'Brien, debuted in 2010. Comedy Central's *The Daily Show* and *The Colbert Report* offer a version of the late-night talk show that focuses heavily on political humor.

Jay Leno (right) jokes with President Barack Obama (left) during a 2012 episode of The Tonight Show with Jay Leno.

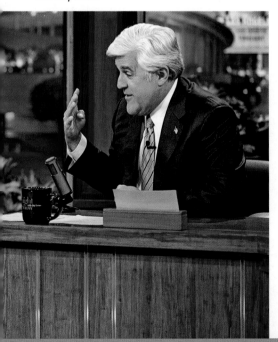

David Letterman opens a 1982 episode of his late-night talk show with a monologue.

THE NEXT GENERATION

Many of today's biggest late-night talk shows have been running for a long time. They are often hosted by the same star for years. When comedian David Letterman retires in 2015, he will have hosted his own late night talk show for more than 30 years, making him the longest-running host in TV history. However, late-night shows do change. In 2014, Jimmy Fallon replaced Leno as host of *The Tonight Show*. Former *Saturday Night Live* star Seth Meyers took over for Fallon as the host of *Late Night*. Letterman's replacement on *The Late Show* will be *The Colbert Report*'s Stephen Colbert. Even though they've been around almost as long as TV itself, these popular shows don't seem to be going away anytime soon. ✴

THE BIRTH OF NETFLIX

Networks and cable channels weren't the only ones to bring television to the Internet. One company that has changed the way people watch TV in recent years is Netflix. Netflix began in 1997 as a service that customers could use to rent DVDs through the mail. In 2007, it began offering subscribers the option to stream movies and TV shows over the Internet instead of waiting for discs to arrive in the mail. Over the following several years, Netflix's streaming service became far more popular than its mail-order disc rentals.

For a low monthly fee, subscribers have unlimited access to thousands of films and TV episodes. They can access this content using television sets, video game consoles, smartphones, computers, and many other devices. As a result of Netflix's popularity, companies such as Hulu, Amazon, and Redbox have launched their own streaming services. Some viewers use these services in addition to their cable or satellite subscriptions, while others have given up traditional television entirely.

Netflix and other streaming services allow people to watch movies and TV shows on almost any device that can connect to the Internet.

Jason Bateman (left) stars in the Netflix series Arrested Development, *narrated by executive producer Ron Howard (right).*

ORIGINAL PROGRAMMING

Streaming services helped change the way people think about watching TV. Previously, viewers had to wait a week or more in between episodes of a favorite show. With streaming services, customers could watch episode after episode whenever they liked.

During the 2010s, streaming services such as Netflix and Amazon began producing their own original TV shows. Many of these series offer the same high quality that viewers are used to seeing on cable channels. Streaming series such as the political drama *House of Cards*, the offbeat sitcom *Arrested Development*, and the thriller *Hemlock Grove* were big hits. In 2013, these three programs became the first Internet-only TV shows to be nominated for Primetime Emmy Awards.

It takes a team of people with different skills and talents to produce a quality television show.

CHAPTER THREE

CAREERS IN TELEVISION

No one person can create a television program alone. It takes a collaborative effort to plan and record the content, edit it, and then broadcast it to a viewing audience. If you flip through the channels, you'll see a wide variety of on-screen talent, from actors and game show hosts to newscasters and sports announcers. In addition to these people, there are countless others working behind the scenes to bring you the programs you love. In the control booth and on the studio floor, there are directors, producers, and a host of technicians. Everyone, from executive producers and directors to production assistants, has a specific job to do. They must all work together if the show is to be successful.

DRAMATIC HIGHLIGHTS

1946	1966	1977	1999
Kraft Television Theatre thrills audiences with live broadcasts of dramatic plays.	The first episode of the legendary science-fiction series Star Trek airs.	Roots becomes the most-watched miniseries broadcast at the time.	HBO's The Sopranos debuts, setting new standards for quality drama on television.

Technical schools are a great way to learn about the equipment and computer software used to edit video and audio recordings.

EDUCATION

Breaking into the television industry isn't easy. It takes a lot of hard work and a little luck as well. Getting a degree from the communications department of a college or university is a good idea for anyone interested in the nontechnical side of broadcasting. Communications courses teach students about the different ways information is shared through television and other media. They provide important skills for future producers, writers, and other TV professionals.

If you're interested in technical work, such as operating a camera or editing footage into a completed program, you might consider attending a technical college. Many of these schools offer specialized programs that will teach you the skills you need to make it in the television industry.

LEARNING AS YOU GO

While education is always a good thing, many of the skills needed to make a successful TV show can only come from on-the-job experience. Most major television companies post job openings online. These companies are almost always looking for workers called production assistants. Production assistants handle a variety of basic tasks on the set of a show, such as carrying equipment, answering phones, or delivering notes. While this is not a very glamorous job, it provides an opportunity to see firsthand how television programs are made. It also gives young workers a chance to meet people in the television industry who might be able to help them find jobs and climb the career ladder.

Production assistants earn valuable on-set experience while playing an important role in creating television shows.

Hugh Haynie produced programming for more than four years at WHYY in Philadelphia, Pennsylvania. He is currently an executive producer at Radiate Media, which provides content to TV, radio, and print outlets nationwide.

When did you first realize that you wanted to work in the television industry? In high school, I belonged to the AV (audiovisual) club. The teacher who ran it also operated the school's TV studio, and I was able to work on a local access program we put on the school's cable access channel. It was a combination sports and comedy show that aired twice a month. I also had an older brother who directed

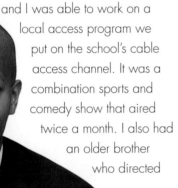

TV commercials, and I went to a few shoots with him. At that time, working in television was fun, but I didn't take it seriously as a career until I went to college.

What kinds of classes did you take in college that prepared you for a career in television? I was a communications major. At that time, the department was called Radio, TV, and Film. It was great because we learned about techniques in all three media. In my junior and senior year, I concentrated on TV and video production. Along the way, I found out that the important thing is to learn how to tell a story well. Once you can do that, you can learn technically how to create a storyline in any media.

What did you learn in other jobs you held in school that helped you in your career? While I was still in school, I videotaped athletic practice and games and dance recitals. The job taught me patience. Videotaping sports requires you to sit still at a camera for a long time, and it can be rather boring. I also learned how to be professional in a work situation with other people.

What was your first job out of school like? My first job was freelancing as a production assistant on film shoots for commercials and feature films. I did everything from carrying lights to getting coffee for the crew.

What television or film project did you work on that you're especially proud of? There are two of them. The first was being the assistant cameraman and editor for a feature film called *Up Against the 8 Ball.* . . . We shot the film in a month in California and Las Vegas, and then I edited it for a couple of months back home. [The second project] was a weekly, half-hour cultural program called *On Canvas* that I produced for WHYY. It consisted of interviews with artists, musicians, and

Hugh Haynie (center) and his WHYY TV crew.

dancers combined with their art or performance. . . . One episode with singer and musician Andrew Bird won a regional Emmy Award. I'm very proud of that.

It takes a team of people to produce a television program. Does working as part of a team come naturally to you, and how do you handle the other team members when you're the producer and the boss? It comes naturally to me. I like the collaborative process and I allow everyone to do their job the best way they know how. I encourage people to speak up. On *On Canvas*, we always voted on the artists we would record.

What advice would you give to a young person who wants to work in television one day? Start creating [your] own content. Practice recording stories with your smartphone. . . . Don't wait until you're in film or video school. Start now. Then learn programming and how to create your own Web site and apps. This will prepare you for the future of television.

Hugh Haynie (left) edits footage for a television show.

LEADING THE TEAM

Television producers hold much of the power and control in a television studio. The executive producer oversees all content and presentation of broadcasts. Each program, however, has its own producer, whether it is a newscast, talk show, documentary, drama, or comedy show. The producer chooses the other members of the team, from the writers and director to the costume designer, set designer, and composer. The producer also provides help as needed with each step of a show's creation.

The director is the person in charge of taking a program from an idea to a finished show. He or she visualizes how the writer's script will appear on the screen. The director rehearses the performers and prepares them for the actual recording that will be broadcast later. He or she often works under intense pressure on a tight deadline for each program.

Producers and directors oversee a show's creation and provide instructions to the other members of the crew.

Thanks to recent advancements in technology, there are a variety of ways to watch your favorite TV shows.

ADVANCING THE TELEVISION EXPERIENCE

The finished product of any television show would be very different without modern technology. Engineers and inventors are constantly improving the way television shows are recorded by companies and accessed by the public. Some develop better cameras or find ways to make filming and broadcasting shows more efficient. Other recent advancements have made it easier than ever to watch television on smartphones and tablets. Some engineers are even working on new and more accurate programs to help you decide what to watch.

These developers often work for broadcasting corporations, such as HBO or Time Warner Cable. Others work for technology companies, such as Apple and Sony Electronics.

THE ARTISTIC SIDE

Some sets might be designed to catch viewers' eyes as they flip through channels.

ARTFUL EFFORTS

The television industry relies heavily on talented artists to help bring shows to life. Words bring across a TV series' story or ideas. Music, costumes, and sets all help to create the overall look and feel of a series. Writers, art directors, costume designers, composers, and other skilled creative professionals all bring their own particular styles, tastes, and ideas to the job.

WORD BY WORD

Scriptwriters write teleplays for dramas and comedies. Reality show writers may write narration to connect unscripted scenes, while late-night talk show writers might write the host's opening comedy routine. Writers at small local TV stations write commercials for businesses that advertise on the station and create the station's promotional material. News writers and news producers use information from news services and write the stories that will be read by the news anchor.

A FEAST FOR THE EYES

The art director is responsible for the scenery on a program. The look of a set is carefully considered for every show, whether it takes place in an office building or a space station. The art director might work with location scouts to find the perfect place to shoot a scene. He or she might also work with artists and craftspeople to build sets from scratch. Furniture and other decorations are chosen for each set or location. On some shows, even the tiniest details might receive close attention from the art director. For example, the art director might choose each and every object placed on a character's desk in a workplace sitcom. These objects might reveal something about the character or provide opportunities for jokes.

DRESSING UP

The costume designer chooses or creates clothing for actors and other performers to wear on-screen. On news programs or talk shows, the costume designer might choose clothing to make the anchors or hosts look friendly and trustworthy. For a drama that is set decades in the past, the designer might research the era to create or obtain clothes that reflect the time period accurately. If the show is a modern-day comedy, the costume designer might try to provide clothes that fit each character's occupation or lifestyle.

LET THERE BE MUSIC

Composers write music for television programs. This music might be a brief, memorable theme for a talk show. Or it might be background music for an hour-long dramatic series. Music is often written after a program has already been shot. The composer watches each scene and writes music that fits the mood the director is trying to convey. Once the music is written, it is performed by musicians and recorded. ✳

Costume designers ensure that actors and other on-screen talent have clothing that fits well and suits their roles on a show.

Newscasters do not have time to memorize lines before their shows are recorded.

MAKE WAY FOR THE TALENT

The people who actually appear on your television screen are usually referred to as the talent. These include actors, performers, commercial spokespersons, and news anchors and reporters. Actors in drama or comedy shows learn their lines from a script, which they may have to memorize in only a few days or less. There is only a brief time to rehearse and record the episode. News anchors and reporters, on the other hand, often rely on notes or **teleprompters** to help them remember what to say.

LIGHTS! CAMERA! ACTION!

Television could not exist without skilled technicians to operate the high-tech equipment used to make shows. Camera operators are responsible for shooting video footage. For most shows, the footage is recorded and then later edited into a final program. For live shows, such as sporting events or most news programs, the footage is broadcast right as the camera operators shoot it. There may be three or more cameras recording the action from different angles.

A lighting designer sets the lights to illuminate the studio stages and create the right mood for each program. For example, comedy shows are usually filmed on bright, well-lit sets, while many dramatic shows might have a darker look. A video engineer operates the video recorder and playback for when a program is broadcast. A studio engineer is responsible for watching over all the equipment and its usage.

Camera operators must stay up to date with the latest video recording technology.

DISPLAY SHOWS WHAT CAMERA IS RECORDING

HANDLES ALLOW OPERATOR TO MOVE THE CAMERA SMOOTHLY

It takes a lot of work to bring a TV series such as The Big Bang Theory to the screen.

4

FROM IDEA TO BROADCAST

Putting together a television program takes a lot of planning and hard work. The creators of a TV show do not have unlimited resources to work with. They must meet deadlines and follow budgets in order for their program to be a success.

Each kind of program has its own unique set of challenges and demands. Dramas and sitcoms have far different requirements than newscasts and documentaries. A show might have a new episode each week, while another has a new episode almost every day. Shows might be long or short, completely scripted or partially improvised, with big casts or just a host or two. Even the most basic programs, such as local talk shows, require a team of creative and technical specialists to successfully bring them to the screen.

KEEP TALKING

1948	1962	1986	2014
The Ed Sullivan Show *debuts* on CBS.	*Johnny Carson begins his long run as host of* The Tonight Show.	The Oprah Winfrey Show *debuts on national television.*	*Jimmy Fallon replaces Jay Leno as host of* The Tonight Show.

A pilot episode gives TV creators a chance to prove that their ideas can become successful television series.

FINDING A CONCEPT

Like all creative projects, a new television show begins with an idea. Depending on the type of show being created and where the show's funding is coming from, this idea could come from a number of different places. A group of top CBS executives might decide that their network needs a new reality program. A famous filmmaker might pitch an idea for a new drama to a cable channel. Or a small, local TV station might decide to create a talk show dealing with important local and state issues.

Once the basic idea for a show is determined, it is time to begin developing the details. For most types of shows, the creators begin by filming a **pilot** episode. This episode is shown to network executives, who then decide if they want to make it into an ongoing series.

GATHERING THE TALENT

Before a show can be made, a full cast and crew of TV professionals must be assembled. For some shows, this could involve hiring hundreds of people. The producers search for workers who are a perfect fit for the kind of show they want to make. Most shows have an entire team of writers who work together to create the scripts for each episode. Some shows have a single director who works on every episode, while others hire many different directors to work on the series.

TV creators might have a certain person in mind to host a talk show or star in a new drama. Other times, they hold auditions and select their cast members from a pool of available talent. For some shows, networks might test potential cast members to make sure they will be appealing to audiences. For others, the show's creators might have the final say in who will be cast.

During an audition, actors read their lines as a show's creators observe the performance.

WHERE THE MAGIC HAPPENS

The cast and creators of the hit drama Breaking Bad *celebrate their victories at the 2013 Primetime Emmy Awards.*

THE ACADEMY OF TELEVISION ARTS & SCIENCES

The Academy of Television Arts & Sciences was created "to promote creativity, diversity, innovation and excellence through recognition, education and leadership in the advancement of the telecommunications arts and sciences." Founded in 1946, just one month after the beginning of network television, the academy has more than 18,000 members in every area of the television industry.

RECOGNIZING THE BEST

To most television viewers, the academy is best known for hosting the Primetime Emmy Awards each year. These awards are one of the biggest honors in the television industry. Actors, producers, directors, and other television pros gather for the star-studded ceremony.

The academy also gives out awards to other television professionals at the annual Creative Arts Emmys, Engineering Emmys, and Television Academy Honors. In addition, it operates the Television Academy Hall of Fame, which recognizes the careers of the industry's biggest legends.

TEACHING TEACHERS

The academy has a foundation that runs several educational programs for students hoping to make it in the television industry. The foundation's annual faculty seminar brings college professors in the television field from all over the country to Los Angeles for five days. During their visit, they participate in discussions, watch presentations, and interact with television professionals to learn more about the industry. They can then use the things they learn to better inform their students. The foundation also sponsors a summer **internship** program. This program offers college students the opportunity to get firsthand industry experience by working directly with professionals from such networks as CBS, HBO, and the Disney Channel. ✳

The Engineering Emmy Awards honor the biggest technological achievements in television each year.

SETTING THE STAGE

Once the cast and crew have been assembled, there is a lot to do before the show can begin filming. The writers and directors begin planning out the episodes to come. The art director works with set designers to create the different sets needed for the show. This might be as simple as setting up a stage with a desk and chairs for a local talk show or as complex as building and decorating several sets for a drama or a sitcom. Costume designers work on the clothing the stars will wear. A composer might start working on an opening theme song for the show, or the show's creators might choose a song that already exists. The show's art department creates graphics for the opening and closing credits.

Some TV shows have sets that are designed to look comfortable and casual.

Rehearsals give sound engineers a chance to make sure audio equipment is adjusted properly before a show is recorded.

INTO THE STUDIO

With everything else in place, the cast and crew can begin preparing to film the show's first episodes. Whether the show is a live talk or sketch comedy show or a carefully shot and edited drama, this process usually begins with rehearsals. Rehearsals can be very different from show to show. While dramatic programs may require several rehearsals, a talk show usually will have only one. Technicians will take readings of visuals and sound. Depending on the production schedule, the rehearsal may take place right before the program is recorded or broadcast live.

Makeup artists might adjust a performer's makeup during commercial breaks or in between takes.

SHOWTIME

On the day of the recording, lighting and microphones are set up ahead of time in the studio. Any last-minute adjustments to the set or costumes are made. Technicians make sure all of the recording equipment is ready to go. Makeup artists apply makeup to the performers. Even on shows such as news programs or talk shows, everyone appearing on camera must wear makeup. The makeup is necessary to make the people look natural under the bright studio lights.

Finally, everyone takes his or her place on the set. The director gives the signal, and filming finally begins. For a comedy or drama show, the director offers instructions to the actors and crew members. The team might shoot scenes several times to make sure they are just right and to get footage from different angles.

UNDER CONTROL

For many other types of shows, the director often works from a control room. The control room contains all the equipment necessary to control and record the program. This includes a bank of monitors on which the director can watch several different camera feeds. From here, the director can issue commands to the camera operators and other technicians. Cameras can be moved around to get a better view, and live broadcasts can switch from one camera to another.

In the control room, sound engineers record the sound and video engineers run the video recording equipment. On stage, performers wear tiny microphones around their necks or attached to their clothing. If a mistake is made during the recording, the director may stop the show and ask the performers to repeat that moment. The mistake will later be edited out of the finished tape. For live broadcasts, this is not an option. The performers must recover from the mistake and move on with the show.

Control room technicians wear headsets and microphones so they can communicate with directors or other crew members on the set.

LASTING CONTRIBUTIONS

READ YOUR LINES

If you are in the studio audience during the recording of a TV show, you might notice the performers glancing offstage at cue cards from time to time. These low-tech inventions are nothing more than poster-size sheets of card stock with lines written on them in black marker. Stagehands stand where the cameras can't see them and hold the cards up for the talent to read. Cue cards may be simple, but they have been helping TV performers remember their lines for decades.

TAKING THEIR CUE

Cue cards are especially popular with late-night talk show hosts and actors on comedy shows such as NBC's *Saturday Night Live*. These shows are broadcast live. This means that if the performers mix up their lines, there is no way to fix the mistake before it is broadcast. In addition, these shows are broadcast weekly or even daily. Performers do not have much time to memorize their lines for each episode.

A crew member reviews cue cards with a talk show host before filming begins.

Cue cards can be a real lifesaver for a performer who needs a quick reminder of what to say next. A talk show host will be able to read his or her opening monologue on the cards if he or she forgets a joke. Sketch comedy cast members can refresh their memories as they perform skits.

CUE CARDS VS. TELEPROMPTERS

Even though most TV studios are now equipped with teleprompters, which can scroll a performer's lines across a screen electronically, many shows still use cue cards instead. This is because they actually offer important benefits over the more modern technology.

Teleprompters are usually placed in front of a camera so a performer can look directly at the lens as he or she reads the lines.

A teleprompter cannot be moved around. This means a performer must face in one direction at all times to keep an eye on the screen. Cue cards are mobile and can be displayed from almost anywhere on the set. Performers also tend to feel more natural and spontaneous when looking at a cue card than they do when reading off a teleprompter. They can look over the entire cue card, while the teleprompter only shows a few lines at a time. Cue cards have been around since almost the beginning of television, and they will probably be around for many more years to come. ✳

CUT AND PASTE

After the recording is wrapped up, the performers and many of the technicians are finished. But the director's work is not over. With the help of editors, he or she will begin assembling the recorded footage into a finished show. There are many things for the director and editors to consider as they work. They need to give the show an interesting look that will appeal to viewers. They also need to make sure the different scenes or segments of the show are in the right order. Finally, they must make cuts to ensure that the show is the right length for its assigned time slot.

In addition to editing, music and any necessary special effects are added during this stage of production. Soon, the edited footage begins to resemble a completed TV episode. Network executives, producers, or other creators watch the show. They might ask for certain changes to be made. Finally, the show is ready to air.

An editor assembles video and audio recordings into a final program.

All of a TV crew's work pays off when their show finally reaches an audience.

SELLING THE SHOW

In the months and weeks leading up to a new show's debut, the network begins advertising to get the word out and drum up interest. For a small, local show, this might be as simple as commercials aired during the channel's other programs or ads in local newspapers. For a major new cable drama, you might see the show's stars displayed on billboards or the sides of buses. You will probably notice online advertisements or see the show's creators appear on popular talk shows.

Finally, the big day comes and the show hits the airwaves for the first time. With any luck, the show will find a loyal audience who will keep watching new episodes and tell their friends about it. If it is a big enough hit, it could run for years and years. And even after it goes off the air, the show might continue to entertain people who enjoy it on discs or streaming services, just as people today continue to enjoy programs that first hit the airwaves decades ago.

THE FUTURE

Today, it is easy to watch television shows anytime and anywhere.

THE FUTURE

Television is changing all the time. The growth of Internet streaming and portable devices such as smartphones and tablets is changing the very nature of broadcasting. It is difficult to predict how television will continue to change in the coming years, but here are some trends that might be coming our way in the not-so-distant future.

ONLINE ONLY

More and more people are choosing to watch television programming online instead of through cable connections or over-the-air broadcasts. The ability to pick and choose what you want to watch, when you want to watch it, and what device you want to watch it on makes online viewing a tempting choice for many people. In addition, more and more new shows are being released exclusively online. They cannot be seen on traditional TV networks or cable channels.

INDEX

Page numbers in *italics* indicate illustrations.

Academy of Television Arts & Sciences, 48, 49
advertising, 39, 57
Alda, Alan, *18*
American Broadcasting Company (ABC), 11, 18, 29
analog television, 23
apps, 37, *59*
Arrested Development, 31, *31*
art departments, 40–41, 50
audiences, 12, 13, 39, 47, 54, 57, *57*
auditions, 47, *47*

Baird, John Logie, 8, 9, 14
Bateman, Jason, *31*
Beat the Clock, 7
Berle, Milton, *12*
Boone, Richard, *11*
Breaking Bad, 48
Burghoff, Gary, *18*

cable television, 18, 19, 21, 26, 27, 29, 30, 58–59
camera operators, 43, *43*, 53, 55
Carson, Johnny, 45
cathode-ray tube (CRT) screens, 24, *24*
censorship, 26
Colbert Report, The, 29
color television, 14, *14*, 24
Columbia Broadcasting System (CBS), 11, 14, 18, 26, 29, 45, 46, 49
Comedy Central, 29
communications towers, 12

composers, 38, 40, 41, 50
Conan, 29
concepts, 46
control rooms, 53, *53*
costume designers, 38, 41, *41*, 50
costumes, 40, 52
credits, 50
Cronkite, Walter, 17, *17*
cue cards, 54–55, *54*

Daily Show, The, 29
digital television, 23, *23*, 24
directors, 33, 38, *38*, 41, 47, 48, 50, 52, 53, 56

early televisions, *6*, 7, 8, *8*, 9, *9*, 12, 14
editing, 34, 37, *37*, 43, 53, 56, *56*
Ed Sullivan Show, The, 28, *28*, 45
education, 34, *34*, 36, 37
Emmy Awards, 7, 31, 37, 48, *48*, 49

Fallon, Jimmy, 29, 45
Farnsworth, Philo, 9, *9*

Have Gun — Will Travel, 11, *11*
Haynie, Hugh, 36–37, *36*, *37*
high-definition (HD) television, 21, 23, 24
Home Box Office (HBO), 18, 26, 29, 33, 49
Howard, Ron, *31*
Howdy Doody Show, The, 12

I Love Lucy, 13, *13*
Internet, 21, 27, 30, 31, 58
internships, 49

job openings, 35
Johnson, Lyndon, 17

Kennedy, John F., 16, *16*
Korean War, 18
Kraft Television Theatre, 33
Kukla, Fran and Ollie, 14–15, *15*

Late Night, 29
Leno, Jay, 28, 29, *29*, 45
Letterman, David, 29, *29*
Lewis, Jerry, *28*
lighting designers, 43
liquid crystal display (LCD) screens, *20*, 24–25, *24–25*
live broadcasts, 13, 22, 27, 33, 43, 51, 53, 54
location scouts, 40
Lone Ranger, The, 7

makeup artists, 52, *52*
Marconi, Guglielmo, 10, *10*
Mary Tyler Moore Show, The, 18
*M*A*S*H*, 18, *18*
Merman, Ethel, *12*
Meyers, Seth, 29
microphones, 52, 53
music, 28, 40, 41, 56

National Broadcasting Company (NBC), 9, 10–11, 14, 15, *15*, 18, 26, 28, 29, 54

INDEX *(CONTINUED)*

Netflix, 21, 30, *30*, 31, *31*
Nipkow disk, 8, *8*
Nipkow, Paul, 8
Nixon, Richard, 16, *16*

Obama, Barack, *28*
O'Brien, Conan, 29
"on-demand" broadcasts. *See* streaming.
Oprah Winfrey Show, The, 45

pilot episodes, 46, *46*
pixels, 14, 25
plasma screens, *20*, 21, 24, 25, *25*
presidential debates, 16, *16*
producers, *31*, 34, 36–37, 38, *38*, 39, 47, 56
production assistants, 35, *35*, 37
public television, 18

radio, 9, 10–11, *10*, 16
Radio Corporation of America (RCA), 9, 12, 14
rehearsals, 38, 42, 51, *51*
resolution, 12
Roots, 33

Sarnoff, David, 9, 10, *10*, *11*
satellite television, 21, 22, *22*, 30
Saturday Night Live, 29, 54
scanning, 8
scripts, 38, 39, 42, 47, *47*
sets, 35, 40–41, *40*, 43, 50, *50*, 52
Sopranos, The, 26, *26*, 33
sound engineers, *51*, 53
stagehands, 54
Star Trek, 33
streaming, 21, 27, *27*, 30, *30*, 31, 57, 58, *58*, 59
Sullivan, Ed, *28*
Swayze, John Cameron, 7

technical schools, 34, *34*
teleprompters, 42, 55, *55*
Telstar satellite, 21, 22
Texaco Star Theater, 12, *12*
Tillstrom, Burr, *15*
Tonight Show, The, 28, 29, *28–29*, 45
Truman, Harry, 12

videocassette recorders (VCRs), 19, *19*
video engineers, 43, 53
Vietnam War, 17, *17*

Walt Disney Studio, 13
Warner Brothers Studio, 13
What's My Line?, 7
WHYY television station, 37, *37*
World's Fair (1939), 10, *10–11*
World War II, 9, 12
writers, 38, 39, *39*, 47, 50

ABOUT THE AUTHOR

STEVEN OTFINOSKI has written more than 160 books for young readers, including books on the history of television, computers, and rockets. He lives in Connecticut.